Made in the USA
Columbia, SC
09 May 2021

37636430R00121